DE BÉRIOT

METHOD

FOR THE

VIOLIN

(Lehmann)

PART I

Ed. 1005

ISBN 978-0-7935-4363-2

G. SCHIRMER, *Inc.*

DISTRIBUTED BY

HAL•LEONARD®
CORPORATION

7777 W. BLUEMOUND RD. P.O. BOX 13819 MILWAUKEE, WI 53213

EDITOR'S NOTE.

In the present, new, edition of the First Part of de Bériot's Violin Method, my chief aim has been to give English-speaking students a clear and concise version of this celebrated work. The omission of the chapter on Solfeggio, as well as the remarks on "The Attitude," etc., is the result of the firm conviction that not only are such matters best learned, and taught, in the class-room, but also that their treatment, when purely theoretical, generally proves futile.

All minor omissions from the original text were considered desirable on the ground that they could not prove helpful to the student, and, in many cases, would serve only to bewilder him.

GEORGE LEHMANN.

NEW YORK, July, 1899.

14982

AUTHOR'S PREFACE.

The results obtained during more than thirty years, in the education of the pupils whom I have had the pleasure of training, constrain me, in some degree, to publish the fundamental principles of my method of instruction.

This work is the fruit of experience as well as of thought. And inasmuch as these principles have been the means of developing so many talented pupils, the labor involved in satisfying my love of perfection has been amply rewarded.

I take pride in paying tribute to the study of the violin, by presenting a system which is based upon new ideas. Without pretending to have attained all that is possible in the art of teaching, I am convinced that I have materially advanced this art by simplifying the educational process.

The present work is divided into three parts, the first and second of which are devoted to the technics of the instrument; the third, to style. Of late years, violinists have been possessed with the feverish ambition to exhibit extraordinary technical skill, often diverting the instrument from its true mission—the noble mission (of imitating the human voice) which has earned for it the glory of being termed "the king of instruments."

The prestige resulting from the display of prodigious technical attainments is, almost always, acquired at the expense of a beautiful quality of tone, perfect intonation, rhythmical accuracy, and, particularly, purity of style.

The excessive work required to overcome these difficulties is calculated to discourage greatly all amateurs. And the eccentricities which, for an instant, dazzle and fascinate, have not, by far, the charm and attraction of melody. Therefore, it is my intention not only to develop the technics of the violin, but also to preserve its true character: which is, to reproduce and express all the sentiments of the soul.

For this reason, I have taken the music of song as a starting-point, both as a model and a guide. Music is the soul of language, whose sentiment it reveals by means of expansion; just as language assists in comprehending the import of music. Music being essentially a language of sentiment, its melodies are always imbued with a certain poetic sense—an utterance, either real or imaginary, which the violinist must constantly bear in mind, so that his bow may reproduce its accents, its prosody, its punctuation. Briefly, he must cause his instrument to speak.

Yet one word. I will not outline the didactic virtues which my work may be found to contain. It has been my endeavor to assign everything to its proper place, so that every study shall be presented at the proper moment. Earnest thought should guide the pupil in the study of my method, so that, ultimately, he may become, if not a great violinist, at least an artist of taste and considerable ability.

v

14982

GENERAL REMARKS.

The course adopted in the first part of this method aims to neglect not one of the essential elements of violin technics. These elements are presented in brief, melodious forms, in order to disguise their dryness as much as possible and render them attractive to the pupil.

The chief elements of violin-playing consist of the different tonalities, the various positions, the bowing, double-stopping, etc.

I do not wish to give any one of the primary difficulties undue importance. On the contrary, I have endeavored to give them all equal prominence, utilizing only that which is indispensable to practical teaching. Thus, I have not gone beyond keys of four sharps or four flats, so that the pupil may always have at his disposal the open strings, comparison with which will be necessary to insure purity of intonation. Also, I have considered it advisable to stop at the 5th position, believing that to be quite sufficient for this first, elementary part.

That the progress of bowing may be neither slow nor neglected through a uniformity of exercises, I have considered it advisable to vary the character of the scales, without, however, increasing the difficulty of fingering. This need not prevent the pupil from playing all the scales in whole notes whenever the teacher considers this desirable.

TABLE OF THE SIGNS AND WORDS EMPLOYED IN THIS WORK.

⊓	Down-bow.
∨	Up-bow.
p *Piano* or *Dolce*	Soft.
pp *Pianissimo* or *Dolcissimo* . . .	Very soft.
f or *Forte*	Loud.
ff or *Fortissimo*	Very loud.
mf or *Mezzo forte*	Less loud.
◁⊏ *Crescendo* or *Cres.*	Increasing in sound.
▷⊐ *Diminuendo* or *Dim.*	Diminishing in sound.
. . . .	Short, detached bowing.
' ' ' '	Bold, detached bowing from the middle of the bow.
Pizzicato or *Pizz.*	To pluck with the finger.
tr.	Trill.
D. C. *Da Capo*	Repeat from the beginning.
⌢ Slur	All the notes under this sign to be played in one bow.

EXTERIOR PARTS OF THE VIOLIN.

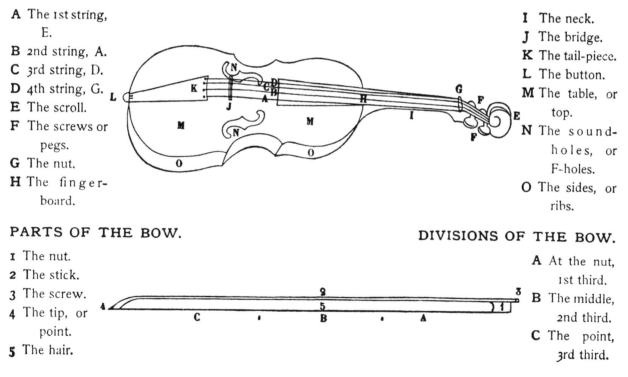

A The 1st string, E.
B 2nd string, A.
C 3rd string, D.
D 4th string, G.
E The scroll.
F The screws or pegs.
G The nut.
H The finger-board.

I The neck.
J The bridge.
K The tail-piece.
L The button.
M The table, or top.
N The sound-holes, or F-holes.
O The sides, or ribs.

PARTS OF THE BOW.

1 The nut.
2 The stick.
3 The screw.
4 The tip, or point.
5 The hair.

DIVISIONS OF THE BOW.

A At the nut, 1st third.
B The middle, 2nd third.
C The point, 3rd third.

Fig. I. A front view of the entire position. Note the turn of the violin to the left, the downward tilt of its right rim, and the horizontal direction of the strings. The left elbow is thrust in front of the breast as required to enable the fingers to govern the tones in the first position on the G-string (a, b, c, d). Two positions of the right arm are drawn, showing the limits of its elevation and depression, as when playing on the outside strings.

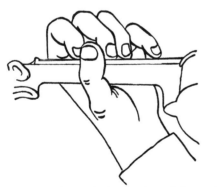

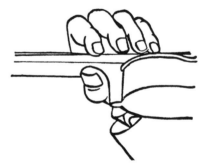

Fig. II. Correct position of the thumb and fingers in the first position, stopping the G-string at a, b, c and d.

Fig. III. Correct position of the thumb and fingers in the fourth position, stopping the G-string at d, e, f and g.

(NOTE.—These cuts are taken from "The Technics of Violin Playing, by Karl Courvoisier."—NEW YORK: G. SCHIRMER.)

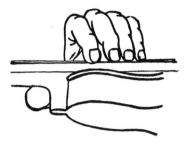

Fig. IV   Correct position of the thumb and fingers in the seventh position, stopping the *G*-string at g, a, b and c.

Fig. V.   Front view of the correct position of the thumb and fingers in the fourth position, stopping the *A*-string at e, f, g and a.

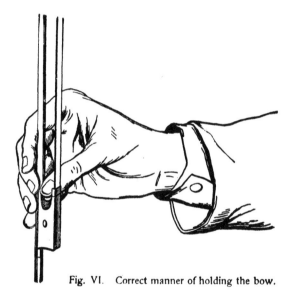

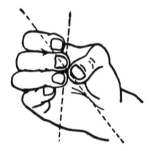

Fig. VI.   Correct manner of holding the bow.

Fig. VII.   Showing the relative positions of the thumb and fingers.

(NOTE.—These cuts are taken from "The Technics of Violin Playing, by Karl Courvoisier."—NEW YORK: G. SCHIRMER.)

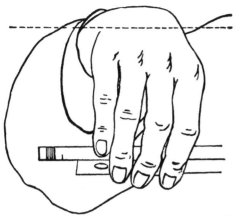

Fig. VIII. Correct position of the hand and wrist showing the parallel between the axis of the joint and the bow.

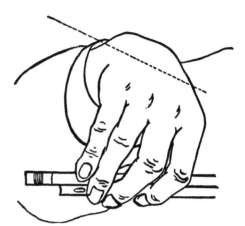

Fig. IX. Incorrect position of the wrist, the hand tilted downward toward the left.

Fig. X. Variations in the position of the right arm in executing a stroke; *a*, at the point of the bow ; *b*, in the middle ; *c*, at the nut. The extremes of the bow are indicated by corresponding letters. The left hand is in the first position, the fingers stopping the *E*-string at *f*, *g*, *a*, *b*.

(NOTE.—These cuts are taken from "The Technics of Violin Playing, by Karl Courvoisier."—NEW YORK: G. SCHIRMER.)

MUSICAL TERMS EMPLOYED IN THIS WORK.

Adagio. A slow movement.

Andante. A moderately slow movement, between Adagio and Allegretto.

Andantino. Slower than Andante (but more often used in the reverse sense).

Allegro. Lively, brisk, rapid.

Allegretto. Moderately fast. Faster than Andante, slower than Allegro.

Animato. Animated, spirited.

Brillante. Brilliant, showy, sparkling.

Cantabile. In a singing manner.

Canto. The vocal or instrumental part (usually the highest) bearing the melody.

Coda. A passage finishing a movement.

Con delicatezza. Refined, delicately.

Con espressione. With expression.

Con sentimento. With feeling, expressively.

Crescendo (cresc.). Increasing the power of tone.

Diminuendo (dim.). Diminishing the power of tone.

Dolce (dol.). Sweet, soft.

Energico. Energetic, vigorous.

Fieramente. Wildly, boldly.

Forte (f). Loud, strong.

Fortissimo (ff). Extremely loud or forcible.

Grazioso. Graceful, elegant.

Largamente. In a broad manner.

Lento. Slow. A tempo between Andante and Largo.

Maestoso. Majestic, dignified.

Maggiore. Major.

Moderato. At a moderate rate of speed.

Piano (p). Soft.

Pianissimo (pp). Very soft.

Più. More.

Poco. A little.

Rallentando (rall.). Gradually growing slower

Risoluto. Energetic, strongly marked.

Sempre. Always, continually.

Semplice. Simple, unaffected.

Sostenuto (sost.). Sustained, prolonged.

Spianato. Even, tranquil.

Preparatory Exercises
in
Bowing on the Open Strings.

The first difficulty experienced in the employment of the bow is to avoid a scraping sound produced by the weight of the wrist on the strings — more especially in the up-stroke when the hand approaches the violin.

This is corrected by utilizing only a small quantity of the hair, conducting the bow with uniform pressure both in the down- and the up-stroke, and by inclining it slightly towards the fingerboard.

A pause should be observed after each note, so that the teacher may correct the position of the arm, the wrist and the fingers.

1st Lesson.

Printed in the U.S.A. by G. Schirmer, Inc.

Preparatory Exercises
for
The Left Hand.

The fingers should be held in readiness for playing, poised above the strings at a distance of about one inch. This will enable them to fall with precision and elasticity.

2nd Lesson.

Moderato.

Printed in the U.S.A. by G. Schirmer, Inc.

Down bow ⊓
Up bow V

When touching the string, the fingers must assume neither a flat nor a perpendicular position. They should be nicely curved, so as to avoid contact with adjacent strings and the interruption of their vibration.

3rd Lesson.

14982

Sustained Tones.

Before beginning the scales, the pupil's attention must be directed to a fault against which he should constantly be on his guard. At the termination of the stroke, in sustained tones, he is generally affected with a nervous impulse to begin the new stroke before the completion of the preceding one. Thus:

4th Lesson.

Defective Bowing.

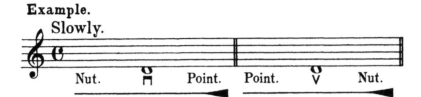

This fault can be remedied by slightly accentuating the **beginning** of the stroke, and by diminishing its speed towards the termination of the tone. Thus:

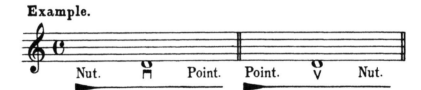

To acquire pure intonation, it is necessary to compare the note produced, with the open strings. The notes D, A and E are, therefore, repeated; so that, playing one with the fourth finger and the other with the open string, faulty intonation can always be rectified.

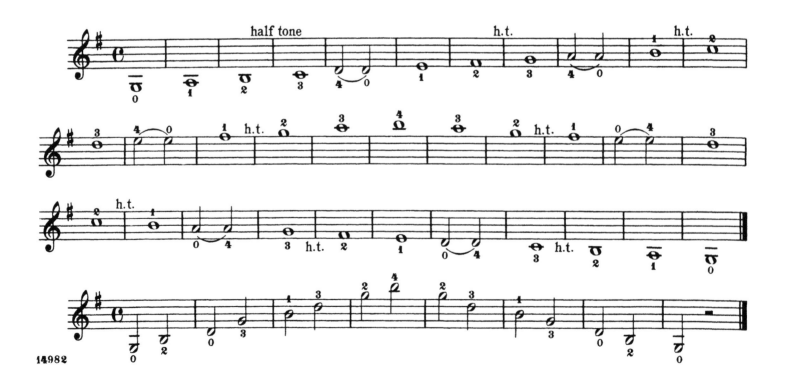

5th Lesson.

Employment of the Fingers

in

Ascending and Descending Scales.

Either in ascending or descending the scales, the employment of the fingers is regulated by the scales themselves. But when the latter extend over several strings, the fingers must abandon their positions successively, and prepare to fall upon the next string.

If, however, the notes of the ascending scale are to be repeated in the *descending* scale (on one string) the fingers must remain on the string to insure perfect intonation and also to avoid unnecessary activity. But these observations apply only to passages requiring a certain degree of rapidity, as in the following illustration.

But in playing very long notes, the application of this principle would only result in the useless expenditure of pressure and energy, and might possible cramp the hand.

If, after playing the scale beginning G-A-B-C-D-, we are to return to the first finger, on A, it is this finger that must be kept in place.

If we are to return to the **second** finger, it is this finger that must remain on the string.

Likewise the third finger:

Example.

The Scale in conjunction with Sharp, Detached Bowing.

Draw the bow from the nut to the point, rapidly and energetically. A pause must be made after each stroke, during which all pressure must be released and the bow remain perfectly motionless on the string.

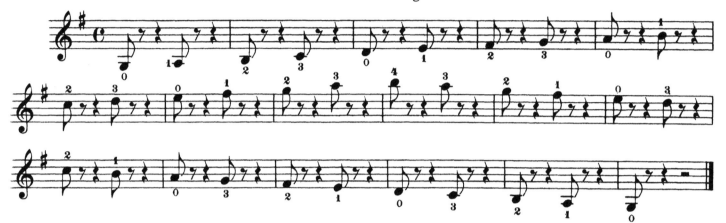

The 1st Position.

These preliminary scales and exercises must be practised slowly, sustaining the notes to their fullest time-value, and without lifting the bow from the strings unless otherwise directed. Keeping the fingers sufficiently close together in the half-tones will be the first difficulty encountered. In order to fix the pupil's attention on this point, these intervals have been indicated, in the first exercises, by the letters "h-t" – (half tone.)

Before beginning a scale, the pupil should curve the fingers nicely, at a distance of about one inch above the string, neither separating them widely nor pressing them close together. The fundamental note must be played in perfect tune before proceeding to the next note.

Scales in the First Position.

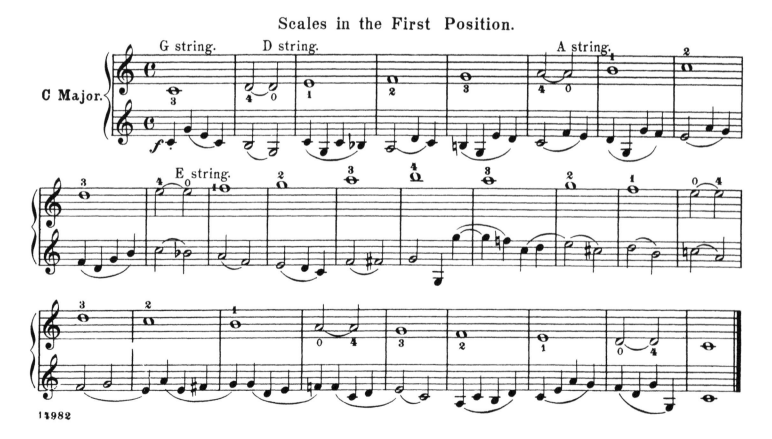

C Major.

A minor.

G major.

E minor.

D major.

B minor.

dolce

n.t.

h.t.

14982

Use the whole bow for each half-note, and only half of the bow for the quarter-notes.

A major.

F♯ minor.

14982

Use the whole bow in the up-stroke.

E major.

Use the whole bow in the down-stroke.

C♯ minor.

14982

The same Scales in flats.

F major.

D minor.

B♭ major.

G minor.

Use the whole bow for the dotted half-notes, and a sixth of the bow – at the point or the nut, as the case may be – for the eighth-notes. Absolute equality of tone must be maintained on the eighth-notes.

E♭ major.

C minor.

The same observations for the following scales as for the two preceding ones.

Ab major.

F minor.

14982

Exercises in the 1st Position.

When passing from one string to another, the pupil must avoid lifting the bow from the strings.

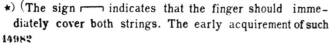

*) (The sign ⌐ indicates that the finger should imme-
diately cover both strings. The early acquirement of such
a habit will prove productive of much good.— Ed.)

First Melody.

Second Melody.

Third Melody.

*) [Wherever two *tempi* are indicated, it is intended that the first one be employed until the pupil is thoroughly familiar with the study in question. But the pupil should ultimately adopt the second *tempo.— Ed.*]

14982

The Slur.

Preparatory Exercises On The Open Strings.

When passing from one string to another, in the same stroke of the bow, it must be done rapidly and accurately, so as to avoid the simultaneous sounding of both strings.

When several notes are slurred in one bow, the fingers alone indicate the progression of the notes, and must therefore be employed with great mechanical precision. The fourth finger, in particular, requires close attention; for, if it is not raised perpendicularly from the string, a disagreeable, drawling sound will invariably ensue.

Fourth Melody.

Fifth Melody.

Sixth Melody.

Moderato. M.M. ♩ = 69. ♩ = 92.

Scales and Exercises in the 2nd Position.

The first condition requisite to obtain a fine quality of tone, is, perfect intonation. This the pupil will acquire by comparing the notes he produces, with the open strings.

In the following scale, the two quarter-notes are to be played with the same stroke of the bow, a pause separating the two, as indicated in the first measure.

Same observation as above.

A pause follows each dotted quarter-note, and the bow should be slightly raised from the string before playing the eighth-notes at the nut of the bow.

Same observation as above.

A pause should follow each dotted quarter-note, and the eighth-notes are played at the point of the bow. Here, however, the bow must remain on the string.

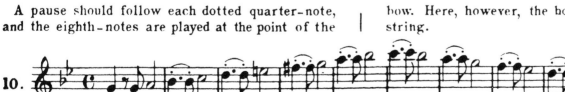

Exercises.

The following exercises in quarter- and eighth-notes must first be practised slowly, and the tone must be sustained throughout the full time-value of the notes. Afterwards, when perfect intonation is attained, the pupil may play these exercises in a faster *tempo,* with rapid and detached bowing, employing the bow between the points A and B, and making a short pause after each note.

First Melody.

14982

Study for bold, detached Bowing.

Second Melody.

14982

Third Melody.
In the 1st and 2nd Positions.

*)[Use the whole bow for the longer notes or where   require **short,** *legato* **strokes.**—*En*⌐
three notes are slurred. The detached eighth-notes
13988

Variation on the preceding Study in the 1st and 2nd Positions.

Allegretto
Broad
1st Pos.

2nd Pos.

Scale in the 3rd Position.

Detach each note at the middle of the bow.

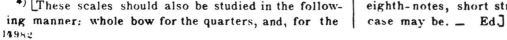

*) [These scales should also be studied in the follow-
ing manner: whole bow for the quarters, and, for the
eighth-notes, short strokes at the point or nut, as the
case may be. — Ed]

14982

The first note of each measure is sharply detached by a rapid stroke of the bow, and is followed by a pause, as indicated in the first measure.

Same observation applied to the last note of each measure.

In this last scale, accentuate strongly the second slurred note.

Exercises in the 3rd Position.

Moderato.

First Melody.

Andante.

Second Melody.

Third Melody.

Fourth Melody.

Allegro maestoso. M.M. ♩=80. ♩=104.

Study in the 1st and 2nd Positions.

40

4th Position.
Scales.

11982

Broad strokes, from the nut towards the point of the bow.

*) [Number 7 should be studied with perfectly loose wrist, at the middle of the bow.- Ed.]

14982
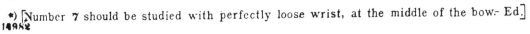

Exercises.

First Melody.

Study.

Second Melody.

Andantino. M.M. ♩ = 66.
♪ = 88.

*) [The first finger must remain on the string. — Ed.]

14982

Allegro moderato. M.M. ♩=80.
♩=100.

Third Melody.

Fourth Melody.
In the 1st, 2nd, 3rd and 4th Positions.

Scales in the 5th Position.

49

14982

First Melody.

In this melody, the pupil should endeavor to play the two sixteenth-notes as lightly and del – | icately at the nut as at the point of the bow.

Second Melody.

Andantino. M. M. ♩ = 66.
♪ = 88.

largamente

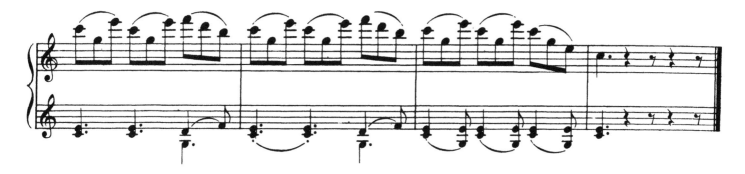

14982

Third Melody.

Moderato. M.M. ♩ = 80.
♩ = 100.

Maggiore.

con sentimento

con anima

Fourth Melody.

In the 1st, 3rd and 5th Positions.

pizz.

14982

arco

pizz.

arco

5th Pos.

Fifth Melody.

In the 1st, 3rd and 5th Positions.

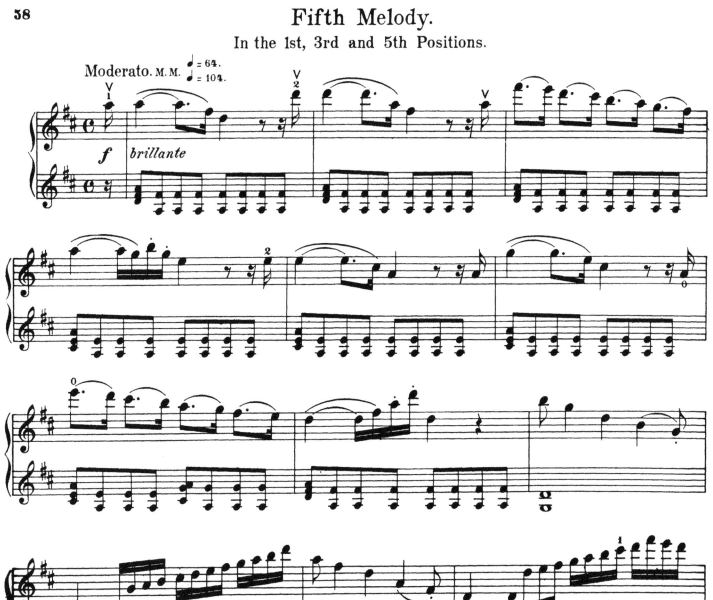

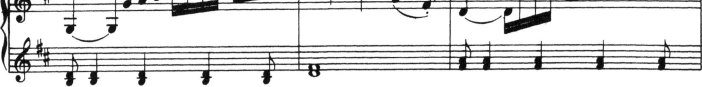

Various kinds of Bowing.

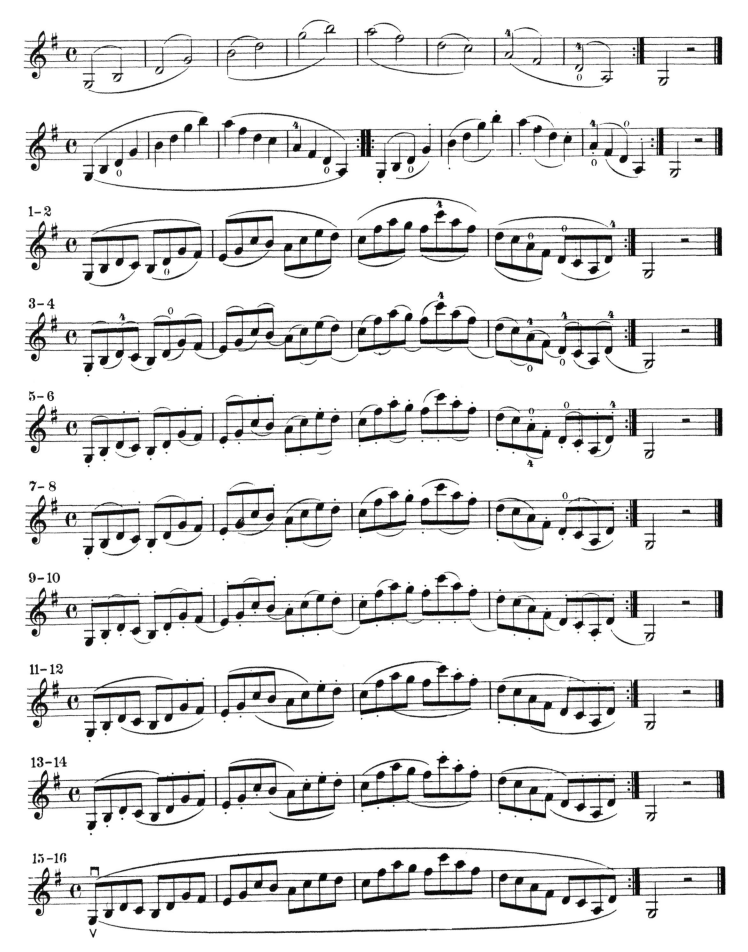

Study
for the
Application of the Various Kinds of Bowing.

Preparatory Exercises.
The Trill.

The value of the notes must be strictly maintained. Let the finger fall from a sufficient height to strike the string firmly and with great precision.

Practise the same scale in the following manner: Also:

Study.
Application of the preceding Exercises.

Note: The following study may first be played in eighth-notes. Thus:

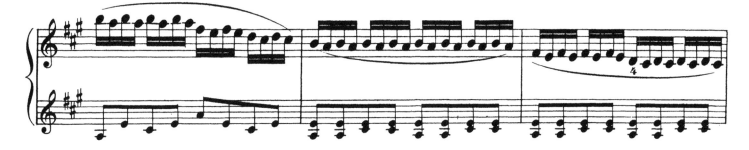

Preparatory Exercises In Double-stopping.

Bowing On Two Open Strings.

Before attempting the study of double-stopping, it is advisable to practise bowing on two open strings. Such preparatory exercise helps the pupil, at the same time, to gradually learn how to tune his instrument. Not only does it require a correct ear to tune a violin well, but it also necessitates much practice.

The pegs have a tendency either to stick fast, or to slip away quite suddenly. It will therefore be found necessary, first to rub them with soap, then, with chalk; after which, they should be turned back and forth in the peg-holes until they are in good working order.

In winding the string on the peg, care must be taken that it does not come in contact with the side of the peg-box and thus hinder its action.

The violin is tuned by sounding the strings with such energy, elasticity and equality of pressure as to obtain their utmost vibration. A violin tuned thus energetically will remain in tune longer than one which has been tuned in a timid manner.

Air and Variations.
Recapitulating the preceding Principles.

67

14982

Più animato.

Coda.

cresc.

f

cresc.

f

mf   *cresc.*

tr   *tr*   *tr*   *tr*

ff